For C, B♭, E♭ & Bass Clef Instruments

SONNY ROLLINS

Play-Along

Trumpet: Jamie Breiwick
Alto and Tenor Sax: Eric Schoor
Piano: Mark Davis
Bass: Jeff Hamann
Drums: David Bayles
Recorded by Ric Probst at Tanner-Monagle Studio

To access online content, visit:
www.halleonard.com/mylibrary

Enter Code
8229-2813-2993-7917

ISBN 978-1-4950-8919-0

7777 W. BLUEMOUND RD. P.O. BOX 13819 MILWAUKEE, WI 53213

For more information on the Real Book series, including community forums, please visit
www.OfficialRealBook.com

Visit Hal Leonard Online at
www.halleonard.com

Contents

Airegin

— SONNY ROLLINS

Blue Seven

— SONNY ROLLINS

Doxy

- Sonny Rollins

C Version

(MED.)

Duke Of Iron

- Sonny Rollins

AFTER SOLOS, D.S. AL ⊕
(PLAY PICKUPS) (TAKE REPEAT)

OLEO

— Sonny Rollins

Pent Up House

— Sonny Rollins

St. Thomas

— Sonny Rollins

Sonnymoon For Two

— Sonny Rollins

C VERSION

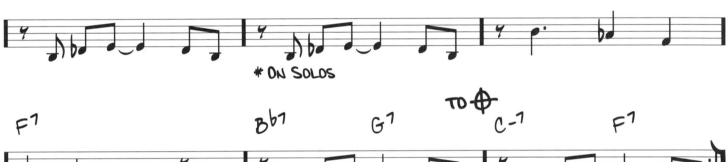

* ON SOLOS

REPEAT HEAD IN/OUT
AFTER SOLOS, D.C. AL ⊕

STRODE RODE

— Sonny Rollins

C VERSION

AFTER SOLOS, D.C. AL FINE
(TAKE REPEAT)

Tenor Madness

— Sonny Rollins

 MED. FAST SWING

C VERSION

AFTER SOLOS, D.S. AL ⊕
(PLAY PICKUP) (TAKE REPEAT)

AIREGIN

— SONNY ROLLINS

AFTER SOLOS, D.C. AL ⊕
(TAKE REPEAT)

Blue Seven

— SONNY ROLLINS

(MED. BLUES)

B♭ VERSION

REPEAT HEAD IN/OUT
AFTER SOLOS, D.C. AL ⊕

Doxy

Bb VERSION

– Sonny Rollins

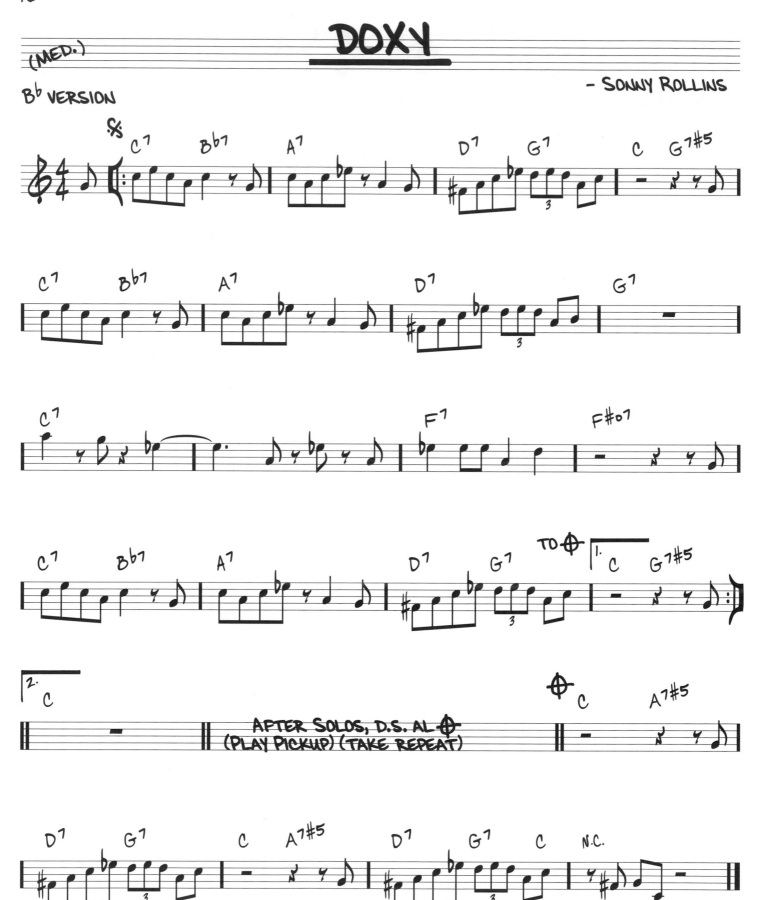

Duke Of Iron

OLEO

— SONNY ROLLINS

Bb VERSION

*SOLO CHANGES

LAST X, FINE
AFTER SOLOS, D.C. AL FINE
(TAKE REPEAT)

Pent Up House

— Sonny Rollins

Sonnymoon For Two

— Sonny Rollins

(MED. SWING)

B♭ Version

* ON SOLOS

REPEAT HEAD IN/OUT
AFTER SOLOS, D.C. AL ⊕

STRODE RODE

– Sonny Rollins

AFTER SOLOS, D.C. AL FINE
(TAKE REPEAT)

Tenor Madness

- Sonny Rollins

B♭ Version

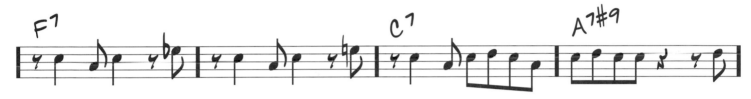

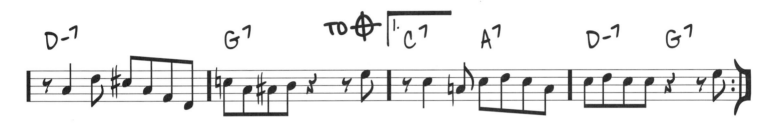

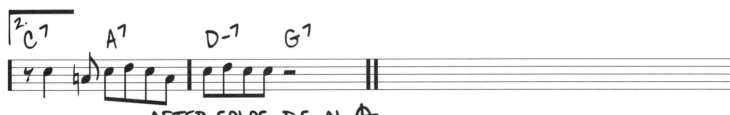

AFTER SOLOS, D.S. AL ⊕
(PLAY PICKUP) (TAKE REPEAT)

AIREGIN

— SONNY ROLLINS

Blue Seven

— Sonny Rollins

Doxy

— Sonny Rollins

(MED.)

Eb VERSION

DUKE OF IRON

OLEO

— Sonny Rollins

(UP)

E♭ Version

LAST X, FINE
AFTER SOLOS, D.C. AL FINE
(TAKE REPEAT)

Pent Up House

— Sonny Rollins

St. Thomas

- Sonny Rollins

SONNYMOON FOR TWO

— Sonny Rollins

(MED. SWING)

E♭ VERSION

* ON SOLOS

REPEAT HEAD IN/OUT
AFTER SOLOS, D.C. AL ⊕

STRODE RODE

– Sonny Rollins

AFTER SOLOS, D.C. AL FINE
(TAKE REPEAT)

TENOR MADNESS

- SONNY ROLLINS

(MED. FAST) SWING

Eb VERSION

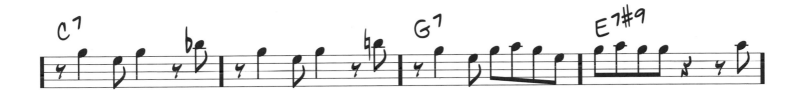
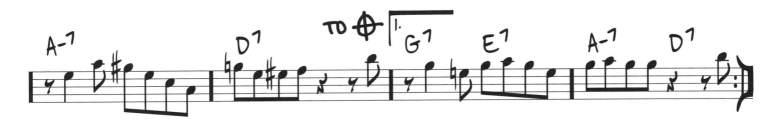

AFTER SOLOS, D.S. AL ⊕
(PLAY PICKUP) (TAKE REPEAT)

Airegin

– Sonny Rollins

Blue Seven

— Sonny Rollins

C BASS VERSION

REPEAT HEAD IN/OUT
AFTER SOLOS, D.C. AL ⊕

DOXY

- Sonny Rollins

C BASS VERSION

(MED.)

Duke of Iron

OLEO

C BASS VERSION

— SONNY ROLLINS

LAST X, FINE
AFTER SOLOS, D.C. AL FINE
(TAKE REPEAT)

Pent Up House

— Sonny Rollins

St. Thomas

— Sonny Rollins

SONNYMOON FOR TWO

— Sonny Rollins

C BASS VERSION

STRODE RODE

– SONNY ROLLINS

AFTER SOLOS, D.C. AL FINE
(TAKE REPEAT)

Tenor Madness

— Sonny Rollins

C BASS VERSION

(MED. FAST SWING)

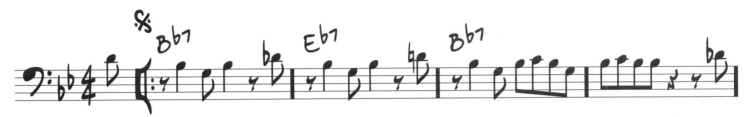

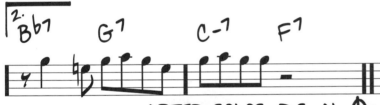

AFTER SOLOS, D.S. AL ⊕
(PLAY PICKUP) (TAKE REPEAT)

THE REAL BOOK MULTI-TRACKS

1. MAIDEN VOYAGE PLAY-ALONG

Autumn Leaves • Blue Bossa • Doxy • Footprints • Maiden Voyage • Now's the Time • On Green Dolphin Street • Satin Doll • Summertime • Tune Up.
00196616 Book with Online Media $17.99

2. MILES DAVIS PLAY-ALONG

Blue in Green • Boplicity (Be Bop Lives) • Four • Freddie Freeloader • Milestones • Nardis • Seven Steps to Heaven • So What • Solar • Walkin'.
00196798 Book with Online Media $17.99

3. ALL BLUES PLAY-ALONG

All Blues • Back at the Chicken Shack • Billie's Bounce (Bill's Bounce) • Birk's Works • Blues by Five • C-Jam Blues • Mr. P.C. • One for Daddy-O • Reunion Blues • Turnaround.
00196692 Book with Online Media $17.99

4. CHARLIE PARKER PLAY-ALONG

Anthropology • Blues for Alice • Confirmation • Donna Lee • K.C. Blues • Moose the Mooche • My Little Suede Shoes • Ornithology • Scrapple from the Apple • Yardbird Suite.
00196799 Book with Online Media $17.99

5. JAZZ FUNK PLAY-ALONG

Alligator Bogaloo • The Chicken • Cissy Strut • Cold Duck Time • Comin' Home Baby • Mercy, Mercy, Mercy • Put It Where You Want It • Sidewinder • Tom Cat • Watermelon Man.
00196728 Book with Online Media $17.99

6. SONNY ROLLINS PLAY-ALONG

Airegin • Blue Seven • Doxy • Duke of Iron • Oleo • Pent up House • St. Thomas • Sonnymoon for Two • Strode Rode • Tenor Madness.
00218264 Book with Online Media $17.99

9. CHRISTMAS CLASSICS

Blue Christmas • Christmas Time Is Here • Frosty the Snow Man • Have Yourself a Merry Little Christmas • I'll Be Home for Christmas • My Favorite Things • Santa Claus Is Comin' to Town • Silver Bells • White Christmas • Winter Wonderland.
00236808 Book with Online Media $17.99

8. BEBOP ERA PLAY-ALONG

Au Privave • Boneology • Bouncing with Bud • Dexterity • Groovin' High • Half Nelson • In Walked Bud • Lady Bird • Move • Witches Pit.
00196728 Book with Online Media $17.99

10. CHRISTMAS SONGS

Away in a Manger • The First Noel • Go, Tell It on the Mountain • Hark! the Herald Angels Sing • Jingle Bells • Joy to the World • O Come, All Ye Faithful • O Holy Night • Up on the Housetop • We Wish You a Merry Christmas.
00236809 Book with Online Media $17.99

The interactive, online audio interface includes:
- tempo control
- looping
- buttons to turn each instrument on or off
- lead sheet with follow-along marker
- melody performed by a saxophone or trumpet on the "head in" and "head out."

The full stereo tracks can also be downloaded and played off-line. Separate lead sheets are included for C, B-flat, E-flat and Bass Clef instruments.

HAL•LEONARD®
www.halleonard.com

HAL•LEONARD® SAXOPHONE PLAY-ALONG

The Saxophone Play-Along Series will help you play your favorite songs quickly and easily. Just follow the music, listen to the audio to hear how the saxophone should sound, and then play along using the separate backing tracks. Each song is printed twice in the book: once for alto and once for tenor saxes. The online audio is available for streaming or download using the unique code printed inside the book, and it includes PLAYBACK+ options such as looping and tempo adjustments.

1. ROCK 'N' ROLL
Bony Moronie • Charlie Brown • Hand Clappin' • Honky Tonk (Parts 1 & 2) • I'm Walkin' • Lucille (You Won't Do Your Daddy's Will) • See You Later, Alligator • Shake, Rattle and Roll.
00113137 Book/Online Audio $16.99

2. R&B
Cleo's Mood • I Got a Woman • Pick up the Pieces • Respect • Shot Gun • Soul Finger • Soul Serenade • Unchain My Heart.
00113177 Book/Online Audio $16.99

3. CLASSIC ROCK
Baker Street • Deacon Blues • The Heart of Rock and Roll • Jazzman • Smooth Operator • Turn the Page • Who Can It Be Now? • Young Americans.
00113429 Book/Online Audio $16.99

4. SAX CLASSICS
Boulevard of Broken Dreams • Harlem Nocturne • Night Train • Peter Gunn • The Pink Panther • St. Thomas • Tequila • Yakety Sax.
00114393 Book/Online Audio. $16.99

5. CHARLIE PARKER
Billie's Bounce (Bill's Bounce) • Confirmation • Dewey Square • Donna Lee • Now's the Time • Ornithology • Scrapple from the Apple • Yardbird Suite.
00118286 Book/Online Audio...$16.99

6. DAVE KOZ
All I See Is You • Can't Let You Go (The Sha La Song) • Emily • Honey-Dipped • Know You by Heart • Put the Top Down • Together Again • You Make Me Smile.
00118292 Book/Online Audio $16.99

7. GROVER WASHINGTON, JR.
East River Drive • Just the Two of Us • Let It Flow • Make Me a Memory (Sad Samba) • Mr. Magic • Take Five • Take Me There • Winelight.
00118293 Book/Online Audio $16.99

8. DAVID SANBORN
Anything You Want • Bang Bang • Chicago Song • Comin' Home Baby • The Dream • Hideaway • Slam • Straight to the Heart.
00125694 Book/Online Audio $16.99

9. CHRISTMAS
The Christmas Song (Chestnuts Roasting on an Open Fire) • Christmas Time Is Here • Count Your Blessings Instead of Sheep • Do You Hear What I Hear • Have Yourself a Merry Little Christmas • The Little Drummer Boy • White Christmas • Winter Wonderland.
00148170 Book/Online Audio $16.99

10. JOHN COLTRANE
Blue Train (Blue Trane) • Body and Soul • Central Park West • Cousin Mary • Giant Steps • Like Sonny (Simple Like) • My Favorite Things • Naima (Niema).
00193333 Book/Online Audio $16.99

11. JAZZ ICONS
Body and Soul • Con Alma • Oleo • Speak No Evil • Take Five • There Will Never Be Another You • Tune Up • Work Song.
00199296 Book/Online Audio $16.99

HAL•LEONARD®

SAXOPHONE
IMPROVE YOUR TECHNIQUE

AMANING PHRASING
50 Ways to Improve Your Improvisational Skills
by Dennis Taylor

Amazing Phrasing is for any sax player interested in learning how to improvise and how to improve their creative phrasing. The ideas are divided into three sections: harmony, rhythm, and melody. The companion audio includes full-band tracks in various musical styles for listening and play along.
00311108 Alto Sax, Book/CD Pack...............$17.99
00310787 Tenor Sax, Book/Online Audio......$16.99

PAUL DESMOND
A Step-by-Step Breakdown of the Sax Styles and Techniques of a Jazz Great
by Eric J. Morones

Examine the sophisticated sounds of a jazz sax legend with this instructional pack that explores 12 Desmond classics: Alone Together • Any Other Time • Bossa Antigua • I've Got You Under My Skin • Jazzabelle • Take Five • Take Ten • Time After Time • and more.
00695983 Book/CD Pack.............................$19.99

JAZZ SAXOPHONE
An In-Depth Look at the Styles of the Tenor Masters
by Dennis Taylor

All the best are here: from the cool bebop excursions of Dexter Gordon, to the stellar musings of John Coltrane, with more than a dozen master players examined in between. Includes lessons, music, historical analysis and rare photos, plus a CD with 16 full-band tracks!
00310983 Book/CD Pack.............................$18.95

MODERN SAXOPHONE TECHNIQUES
by Frank Catalano

Many books present facts, but this guide teaches the developing player how to learn. Listening, exploring, writing original music, and trial and error are some of the methods threaded throughout. On the online video, author and virtuoso saxophonist Frank Catalano offers quick tips on many of the topics covered in the book. Topics include: developing good rhythm • air stream and embouchure • fingering charts • tonguing techniques • modern harmony tips • and more.
00123829 Book/Online Video $24.99

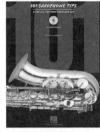

101 SAXOPHONE TIPS
by Eric Morones

This book presents valuable how-to insight that saxophone players of all styles and levels can benefit from. The text, photos, music, diagrams, and accompanying CD provide a terrific, easy-to-use resource for a variety of topics, including: techniques; maintenance; equipment; practicing; recording; performance; and much more!
00311082 Book/CD Pack............................$15.99

SONNY ROLLINS
A Step-by-Step Breakdown of the Sax Styles & Techniques of a Jazz Giant

Explore the unique sound and soul of jazz innovator Sonny Rollins on licks from 12 classic songs: Airegin • Biji • Don't Stop the Carnival • Doxy • Duke of Iron • God Bless' the Child • Oleo • St. Thomas • Sonnymoon for Two • Tenor Madness • Way Out West • You Don't Know What Love Is.
00695854 Book/CD Pack............................$19.99

SAXOPHONE AEROBICS
by Woody Mankowski

This 52-week, one-exercise-a-day workout program for developing, improving and maintaining saxophone technique includes access to demo audio tracks online for all 365 workout licks! Techniques covered include: scales • articulations • rhythms • range extension • arpeggios • ornaments • and stylings. Benefits of using this book include: facile technique • better intonation • increased style vocabulary • heightened rhythmic acuity • improved ensemble playing • and expanded range.
00143344 Book/Online Audio.....................$19.99

THE SAXOPHONE HANDBOOK
Complete Guide to Tone, Technique, and Performance
by Douglas D. Skinner
Berklee Press

A complete guide to playing and maintenance, this handbook offers essential information on all dimensions of the saxophone. It provides an overview of technique, such as breathing, fingerings, articulations, and more. Exercises will help you develop your sense of timing, facility, and sound. You'll learn to fine-tune your reed, recork the keys, fix binding keys, replace pads, and many other repairs and adjustments. You'll also learn to improve your tone, intonation, and flexibility while playing with proper technique.
50449658 ....$14.99

SAXOPHONE SOUND EFFECTS
by Ueli Dörig
Berklee Press

Add unique saxophone sounds to your palette of colors! The saxophone is capable of a great range of sounds, from laughs and growls to multiphonics and percussion effects. This book shows you how to do 19 different inventive effects, with etudes that put them in a musical context. The accompanying online audio provides play-along tracks for the etudes and examples of each sound effect in isolation.
50449628 Book/Online Audio.....................$15.99

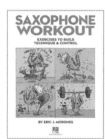

SAXOPHONE WORKOUT
by Eric J. Morones

This book will give you a complete saxophone workout. Here you'll find etudes that cover a wide spectrum of techniques, from the basics to intermeidate level to advanced. With daily practice that includes use of a metronome and tuner, this book will provide noticeable improvement in the mastery of your horn. The excercises are designed for the trouble spots of all the instruments of the saxophone family – soprano, alto, tenor, baritone – and can be used by players at all levels.
00121478 ....$12.99

25 GREAT SAX SOLOS
Transcriptions • Lessons • Bios • Photos
by Eric J. Morones

From Chuck Rio and King Curtis to David Sanborn and Kenny G, take an inside look at the genesis of pop saxophone. This book with online audio provides solo transcriptions in standard notation, lessons on how to play them, bios, equipment, photos, history, and much more. The audio contains full-band demos of every sax solo in the book, and includes the PLAYBACK+ audio player which allows you to adjust the recording to any tempo without changing pitch, loop challenging parts, pan, and more! Songs include: After the Love Has Gone • Deacon Blues • Just the Two of Us • Just the Way You Are • Mercy, Mercy Me • Money • Respect • Spooky • Take Five • Tequila • Yakety Sax • and more.
00311315 Book/Online Audio.....................$19.99

HAL•LEONARD®
www.halleonard.com

Prices, content, and availability subject to change without notice.

0118

HAL•LEONARD INSTRUMENTAL PLAY-ALONG

Your favorite songs are arranged just for solo instrumentalists with this outstanding series. Each book includes a great full-accompaniment play-along audio so you can sound just like a pro! Check out www.halleonard.com to see all the titles available.

The Beatles

All You Need Is Love • Blackbird • Day Tripper • Eleanor Rigby • Get Back • Here, There and Everywhere • Hey Jude • I Will • Let It Be • Lucy in the Sky with Diamonds • Ob-La-Di, Ob-La-Da • Penny Lane • Something • Ticket to Ride • Yesterday.

_____	00225330	Flute	$14.99
_____	00225331	Clarinet	$14.99
_____	00225332	Alto Sax	$14.99
_____	00225333	Tenor Sax	$14.99
_____	00225334	Trumpet.	$14.99
_____	00225335	Horn	$14.99
_____	00225336	Trombone	$14.99
_____	00225337	Violin.	$14.99
_____	00225338	Viola	$14.99
_____	00225339	Cello	$14.99

Chart Hits

All About That Bass • All of Me • Happy • Radioactive • Roar • Say Something • Shake It Off • A Sky Full of Stars • Someone like You • Stay with Me • Thinking Out Loud • Uptown Funk.

_____	00146207	Flute	$12.99
_____	00146208	Clarinet	$12.99
_____	00146209	Alto Sax	$12.99
_____	00146210	Tenor Sax	$12.99
_____	00146211	Trumpet.	$12.99
_____	00146212	Horn	$12.99
_____	00146213	Trombone	$12.99
_____	00146214	Violin.	$12.99
_____	00146215	Viola	$12.99
_____	00146216	Cello	$12.99

Coldplay

Clocks • Every Teardrop Is a Waterfall • Fix You • In My Place • Lost! • Paradise • The Scientist • Speed of Sound • Trouble • Violet Hill • Viva La Vida • Yellow.

_____	00103337	Flute	$12.99
_____	00103338	Clarinet	$12.99
_____	00103339	Alto Sax	$12.99
_____	00103340	Tenor Sax	$12.99
_____	00103341	Trumpet.	$12.99
_____	00103342	Horn	$12.99
_____	00103343	Trombone	$12.99
_____	00103344	Violin.	$12.99
_____	00103345	Viola	$12.99
_____	00103346	Cello	$12.99

Disney Greats

Arabian Nights • Hawaiian Roller Coaster Ride • It's a Small World • Look Through My Eyes • Yo Ho (A Pirate's Life for Me) • and more.

_____	00841934	Flute	$12.99
_____	00841935	Clarinet	$12.99
_____	00841936	Alto Sax	$12.99
_____	00841937	Tenor Sax	$12.95
_____	00841938	Trumpet.	$12.99
_____	00841939	Horn	$12.99
_____	00841940	Trombone	$12.99
_____	00841941	Violin.	$12.99
_____	00841942	Viola	$12.99
_____	00841943	Cello	$12.99
_____	00842078	Oboe	$12.99

Great Themes

Bella's Lullaby • Chariots of Fire • Get Smart • Hawaii Five-O Theme • I Love Lucy • The Odd Couple • Spanish Flea • and more.

_____	00842468	Flute	$12.99
_____	00842469	Clarinet	$12.99
_____	00842470	Alto Sax	$12.99
_____	00842471	Tenor Sax	$12.99
_____	00842472	Trumpet.	$12.99
_____	00842473	Horn	$12.99
_____	00842474	Trombone	$12.99
_____	00842475	Violin.	$12.99
_____	00842476	Viola	$12.99
_____	00842477	Cello	$12.99

Popular Hits

Breakeven • Fireflies • Halo • Hey, Soul Sister • I Gotta Feeling • I'm Yours • Need You Now • Poker Face • Viva La Vida • You Belong with Me • and more.

_____	00842511	Flute	$12.99
_____	00842512	Clarinet	$12.99
_____	00842513	Alto Sax	$12.99
_____	00842514	Tenor Sax	$12.99
_____	00842515	Trumpet.	$12.99
_____	00842516	Horn	$12.99
_____	00842517	Trombone	$12.99
_____	00842518	Violin.	$12.99
_____	00842519	Viola	$12.99
_____	00842520	Cello	$12.99

Songs from Frozen, Tangled and Enchanted

Do You Want to Build a Snowman? • For the First Time in Forever • Happy Working Song • I See the Light • In Summer • Let It Go • Mother Knows Best • That's How You Know • True Love's First Kiss • When Will My Life Begin • and more.

_____	00126921	Flute	$14.99
_____	00126922	Clarinet	$14.99
_____	00126923	Alto Sax	$14.99
_____	00126924	Tenor Sax	$14.99
_____	00126925	Trumpet.	$14.99
_____	00126926	Horn	$14.99
_____	00126927	Trombone	$14.99
_____	00126928	Violin.	$14.99
_____	00126929	Viola	$14.99
_____	00126930	Cello	$14.99

Top Hits

Adventure of a Lifetime • Budapest • Die a Happy Man • Ex's & Oh's • Fight Song • Hello • Let It Go • Love Yourself • One Call Away • Pillowtalk • Stitches • Writing's on the Wall.

_____	00171073	Flute	$12.99
_____	00171074	Clarinet	$12.99
_____	00171075	Alto Sax	$12.99
_____	00171106	Tenor Sax	$12.99
_____	00171107	Trumpet.	$12.99
_____	00171108	Horn	$12.99
_____	00171109	Trombone	$12.99
_____	00171110	Violin.	$12.99
_____	00171111	Viola	$12.99
_____	00171112	Cello	$12.99

Wicked

As Long As You're Mine • Dancing Through Life • Defying Gravity • For Good • I'm Not That Girl • Popular • The Wizard and I • and more.

_____	00842236	Flute	$12.99
_____	00842237	Clarinet	$12.99
_____	00842238	Alto Saxophone	$11.95
_____	00842239	Tenor Saxophone.	$11.95
_____	00842240	Trumpet.	$11.99
_____	00842241	Horn	$12.99
_____	00842242	Trombone	$12.99
_____	00842243	Violin.	$11.99
_____	00842244	Viola	$12.99
_____	00842245	Cello	$12.99

Prices, contents, and availability subject to change without notice.
Disney characters and artwork © Disney Enterprises, Inc.

HAL•LEONARD®